About the Series

It might almost be said that the most enchanting part of baseball lies not in watching it, but in remembering it. No sport lends itself so effortlessly to memory, to conversation; no sport has so graphic an afterlife in its statistics; nor has any been photographed so thoroughly and excitingly.

Beginning with 1901, the year most historians identify as the dawn of baseball's "modern era," there have been nearly 90 seasons, with no two even remotely alike. The mention of a certain year can evoke the memory of a team, the image of a man, or the drama of a moment. For many fans, it is all so vivid that baseball has become for them a long calendar of historical events.

Every season begins the same, with everyone equal on Opening Day, stirring with optimism and anticipation. And every season ends the same way, with surprises and disappointments, among teams and individuals both. No baseball summer has even been, or can be, dull. No baseball summer has ever been forgotten, for every one has been a source of stories and numbers, many of which have become part of our national folklore.

It is the purpose of this series of books to make it all happen one more time.

The Bantam
Baseball Collection

#3

National
League
Rookies
of the
Year

Written by
Donald Honig

Packaged by Angel Entertainment, Inc.
and M.I.B. Baseball Enterprises, Inc.

BANTAM BOOKS
TORONTO · NEW YORK · LONDON · SYDNEY · AUCKLAND

National League Rookies of the Year

A Bantam Book / April 1989

ISBN 0-553-27979-3

PRINTED IN THE UNITED STATES OF AMERICA

0 9 8 7 6 5 4 3 2 1

Contents

Introduction

The Rookie of the Year Award was instituted by the Baseball Writers Association of America (BBWAA) in 1947. For the first two years there was just one winner, selected from both major leagues. In 1949, the process was expanded to choose the outstanding rookie from each league. Three writers from each big-league city participated in the voting, with the number of voters being reduced to two per city in 1961.

In the beginning, the writers were free to use their own interpretation as to what constituted a rookie. It wasn't until 1957 that qualifying guidelines were put down. It was ruled that, during the previous year, more than 75 at-bats, 45 innings pitched, or having been on a big-league roster between May 15 and September 1 would make a player eligible for Rookie of the Year consideration. These stipulations were soon changed to 90 at-bats, 45 innings, or 45 days on the roster before September 1. In 1971, they were amended again to the current 130 at-bats, 50 innings or 45 days service on the roster. In 1980 the current system of voting was introduced: a writer could select three rookies on his ballot, with votes allocated on a 5-3-1 basis, in order of preference. In the National League today, the highest possible number of votes is 120, in the American League, 140. Unanimous selections have been a rarity. By the 1987 season, there were five in the National League: Frank Robinson (1956), Orlando Cepeda (1958), Willie McCovey (1959), Vince Coleman (1985) and Benny Santiago (1987). There were just two in the American: Carlton Fisk (1972) and Mark McGwire (1987).

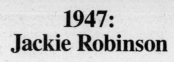

1947:
Jackie Robinson

The first man to win the newly-instituted Rookie of the Year designation was, appropriately enough, the most unique rookie player in baseball history. He had come to the major leagues in a veritable cauldron of pressure, a man who stirred the strongest of passions and evoked the deepest of hopes.

As the person selected by the owner of the Brooklyn Dodgers, Branch Rickey, to break baseball's odious long-standing color barrier, Robinson was faced with myriad problems and challenges. He was trying to succeed in the big leagues, he was reviled and insulted by the opposition and some of his teammates were uncomfortable with him. A naturally combative and outspoken man, he was under strict orders from Rickey to take all abuse passively (lest there be an "incident"). To cap it all, he was breaking in at a position unfamiliar to him—first base. After having played shortstop in the Negro Leagues, Robinson found the only opening available to him on a talented Brooklyn Dodger team was first base, and he played it more than acceptably.

The 28-year-old Dodger rookie responded to his monumental task by playing a dynamic, sometimes electrifying brand of ball. On the basepaths, he was daring and dazzling, leading the league with 29 stolen bases, (more than twice the total of the runner-up); at home plate he was consistent all season, batting .297 and scoring 125 runs, second-best in the league.

As the season wore on, Robinson gradually won the respect and admiration, albeit sometimes grudging, of teammates and opponents alike. Teammate Peter Reiser, who supported Jackie from the beginning, said, "Some of the southern boys had been doubters. They didn't want to play with him. But then they saw how good he was, that he was winning ball games for us, and that he could help us win the pennant and get that World Series money. Then they became believers. Without Jackie, we never would have won the pennant that year."

Placing a close second to Robinson in the voting was another outstanding rookie, New York Giants righthander Larry Jansen who was 21-5. New York Yankee righthander Frank Shea was third. Robinson's greatest achievement that year? According to Dodger coach Clyde Sukeforth, "It was keeping bottled up inside of him his natural militancy and outspokenness. It took a toll on him mentally, but he knew he had no alternative. He was a great crusader, that fellow."

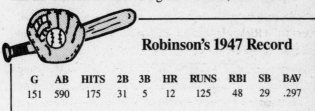

Robinson's 1947 Record

G	AB	HITS	2B	3B	HR	RUNS	RBI	SB	BAV
151	590	175	31	5	12	125	48	29	.297

Jackie Robinson generating the excitement that made him one of the most popular players of his time. Here he is stealing home, just avoiding the catcher's lunge.

After his sensational rookie year, Fernando Valenzuela and the Dodgers were having trouble agreeing on a salary for the next year. Fernando was holding out (this is the time when baseball clubs say that all those statistics their publicity people were bragging about the previous summer weren't really all that good). When manager Tom Lasorda was asked what Fernando was demanding, he said, "I think he wants Texas back."

1948: Alvin Dark

In 1948 there was still a single winner of the Rookie of the Year award, and for the second year in a row the winner was a National Leaguer—Boston Braves shortstop Alvin Dark.

Always known as an intelligent ballplayer and a relentless competitor, Dark had starred in football and baseball at Louisiana State and then entered the Marine Corps. So he was a mature 26-year-old when he took over at short in 1948 for the Braves (who had signed him for a $40,000 bonus, a hefty price tag in those days).

Spearheaded by their gifted and aggressive rookie, the Braves went on to win their first pennant since 1914. Dark earned his Rookie honors with a .322 batting average; among his 175 hits were 39 doubles. Defensively, Alvin was never among the most gifted shortstops, but, like Lou Boudreau (who Dark opposed in the World Series that year), he had a knack for making the clutch play. Somehow he always found the resources to "get up" for that big play and with his straight overhand peg get his man. Dark was a runaway choice for Rookie of the Year, easily beating out Cleveland lefthander Gene Bearden and the Philadelphia Phillies' fine young centerfielder Richie Ashburn.

Dark dropped to .276 in 1949 and the Braves made the mistake of trading him to the Giants. In New York, Alvin helped the Giants to two pennants. After retiring in 1960, the brainy Dark found long employment as a manager, running the San Francisco Giants, Kansas City Athletics, Cleveland Indians, Oakland Athletics and San Diego Padres.

Dark's 1948 Record

G	AB	HITS	2B	3B	HR	RUNS	RBI	SB	BAV
137	543	175	39	6	3	85	48	4	.322

Alvin Dark, Rookie of the Year shortstop and future big league manager.

1949:
Don Newcombe

In the first year that each league made its own selection for Rookie of the Year, the National League winner was Brooklyn Dodger righthander Don Newcombe, winning easily over Del Crandall, the fine young catcher of the Boston Braves.

The 23-year-old Newcombe was a big man, with a full, vigorous windup, out of which he delivered a smoking fastball. Signed out of the Negro Leagues soon after Jackie Robinson, Big Don worked his way up through the Dodger farm system and finally joined the big club in May, 1949.

"He was big and fast and strong," Dodger manager Burt Shotton said, "but what I liked most about him was his control. He had excellent control."

The Dodgers needed one more pitcher in order to make a pennant run in 1949 and Newcombe was that man, with plenty to spare. The rookie took over and quickly became the ace of the staff, ringing up a 17-8 record and tying for the league lead in shutouts. With the Dodgers winning the pennant by one game over the Cardinals, the new man's contribution was, to put it mildly, substantial.

Newk, who fought a successful battle against alcoholism late in his career, went on to greater glory with the Dodgers, winning 20 or more three times, including a whopping 27 in 1956.

Newcombe's 1949 Record

WON	LOST	PCT.	G	GS	CG	INP	HITS	BB	SO	SH	ERA
17	8	.680	38	31	19	244	223	73	149	5	3.17

Don Newcombe, ace pitcher on some of the greatest National League teams of all time.

8

1950: Sam Jethroe

Outfielder Sam Jethroe came to the major leagues with the Boston Braves in 1950 with a reputation for possessing blazing running speed. In 1949, playing for the Dodgers' Montreal club in the International League, he stole 89 bases. With a surfeit of young outfielders, however, the Dodgers sold Jethroe to the Braves and Sam went on to become the National League's Rookie of the Year in 1950, beating out Phillies righthander Bob Miller and Pirates second-baseman Danny O'Connell.

The 26-year-old switch-hitting Jethroe was the Boston Braves' first black player (following the Dodgers and Giants, the Braves were the third National League team to bring up a black. The rest of the teams were pretending nothing was happening). Sam started off well, batting .273, hitting 18 home runs, and leading the league with 35 stolen bases (this may seem like small potatoes today, but in 1950 it was the second highest total in the National League in 21 years).

Jethroe had an even better year in 1951, again hitting 18 homers and stealing a league-leading 35 bases, while batting .280. But soon after that, his career turned to soggy bread. After batting .232 in 1952, he dropped out of the big leagues, resurfaced for two games with the Pirates in 1954 and then left for good.

Why was Sam's career so short? According to one cynic, "In those days, whenever the Dodgers sold a top minor-league prospect, it was because they knew something about him. You notice they didn't sell guys like Duke Snider, Roy Campanella, Don Newcombe, or Carl Erskine." Which leads one to believe that in the Dodger front office in those years there were dossiers labeled "Classified."

Jethroe's 1950 Record

G	AB	HITS	2B	3B	HR	RUNS	RBI	SB	BAV
141	582	159	28	8	18	100	58	35	.273

His flashing speed earned the nickname "Jet" for Boston's Sam Jethroe.

1951: Willie Mays

Unlike 1950's National Rookie-of-the-Year Sam Jethroe, 1951's designee came to stay. His name was Willie Mays, and in late May the New York Giants brought the 20-year-old center fielder up from their Minneapolis farm club, where he was batting .477. He started slowly, doing nothing for his first 12 at-bats, before finally launching a rocket shot off of the great Warren Spahn at the Polo Grounds. The ball soared over the left-field roof, a herald shot if ever there was one. It was followed by 659 others before Willie's retirement in 1973.

Mays joined a floundering Giant club and with the timeliness of his hitting, the almost theatrical splendor of his defensive play, and the carbonated verve of his personality, he helped drive them to the storybook pennant, which was won by Bobby Thomson's home run against the Dodgers in the ninth inning of the final game of a three-game playoff.

In the Rookie-of-the-Year voting, Willie was an easy winner over Braves lefthander Chet Nichols (the ERA leader) and the Dodgers' Clem Labine. Though Willie's opening-year stats were not thunderous, they were substantial enough—.274 batting average and 20 home runs.

The glittering rookie of 1951 was to evolve into what many people considered the greatest player of the post-war era (meaning since the young DiMaggio). Willie enchanted as many people with his bubbly personality as with his ball playing; Branch Rickey once said about him, "The secret weapon is the frivolity in his bloodstream. Willie Mays has doubled his strength with laughter." In retirement, however, the Mays personality seemed to some writers less appealing. Journalistic potshots at him included the words, "grouchy," "surly," "selfish." Well, they also said that DiMaggio was "aloof," Williams "testy," and Mantle "sullen." They also complained that Musial smiled too much. It all means that if you are a prince in the universe of baseball, people take notice of you.

Mays' 1951 Record

G	AB	HITS	2B	3B	HR	RUNS	RBI	SB	BAV
121	464	127	22	5	20	59	68	7	.274

Willie Mays taking his rips.

Willie Mays.

1952: Joe Black

The year before, the Brooklyn Dodgers had seen a 13 1/2 game lead in mid-August evaporate like an ice sculpture, melting drop by drop, until being swept completely away by the hurricane force of Bobby Thomson's home run. After the season, Brooklyn's ace pitcher, Don Newcombe, had been drafted. Nevertheless, the disheartened, suddenly pitching-poor club regrouped, rearmed, and went on to take a pennant in 1952 that was won fairly easily.

The man who made the difference for the Dodgers in 1952 was a 28-year-old right-handed rookie reliever who wasn't even on the team's roster in spring training. But Joe Black made the team, primarily, according to manager Charlie Dressen, "Because he had a good fastball and because we had lost Don Newcombe."

Black became the Dodger bullpen. Firing a good fastball and a tight-breaking curve, he appeared in 56 games (54 of them in relief), winning 15 and saving 15 (the save, a latter-day statistical invention, was computed retroactively). And Joe pitched with authority; in those more free-wheeling days, he was not averse to flattening batters who crowded him. By mid-season, it was becoming more and more apparent that when Joe Black took over in the late innings, the game was over.

Black swept the Rookie of the Year voting, easily beating out runner-up Hoyt Wilhelm, the Giants' knuckleballing reliever who had been just as impressive coming out of the bullpen for the Giants as Black had been for the Dodgers. Black had 19 votes, Wilhelm 3, and drawing one vote apiece were a couple of rookies who were going to get better and better—Pirates shortstop Dick Groat and Braves third baseman Eddie Mathews.

Black's 1952 Record

WON	LOST	PCT.	G	GS	CG	INP	HITS	BB	SO	SH	ERA
15	4	.789	56	2	1	142	102	41	85	0	2.15

Joe Black, Brooklyn's spectacular 1952 rookie reliever.

1953: Jim Gilliam

Reflecting baseball's new era, and for the fifth year in a row, the National League's Rookie of the Year was a black player. This time it was Brooklyn's switch-hitting second baseman Jim Gilliam, a solid, versatile player destined to have a long career with the Dodgers in both Brooklyn and Los Angeles.

Gilliam batted .278 and led the league with 17 triples. Nicknamed "Junior," the new man was impressive enough to easily out-poll the Cardinals' rookie lefthander Harvey Haddix, who was 20-9 and led the league with six shutouts. Another Cardinal newcomer, third baseman Ray Jablonski, who had 112 runs batted in, finished third.

Gilliam's emergence moved Jackie Robinson from second base to splitting his time between third and left field, enabling the Dodgers to field one of the most powerful units in National League history: Roy Campanella catching, Gil Hodges at first base, Gilliam, Pee Wee Reese at shortstop, Robinson (or Billy Cox) at third, and Robinson, Duke Snider and Carl Furillo in the outfield. This club led the league in batting, slugging, runs, hits, home runs, and stolen bases, as they won 105 games and coasted to an easy pennant.

The Rookie of the Year scored 125 runs, one of six Dodgers to score over 100 runs that year, tying the major-league record.

Gilliam's 1953 Record

G	AB	HITS	2B	3B	HR	RUNS	RBI	SB	BAV
151	605	168	31	17	6	125	63	21	.278

Jim Gilliam, one of Walter Alston's favorite players.

1954: Wally Moon

The sixth-place St. Louis Cardinals led the National League in batting in 1954 with a .281 team average. Among the seven .280-plus hitters the Cardinals had in their lineup was their Rookie of the Year outfielder, Wally Moon. The blossoming of the 24-year-old Moon led some St. Louis sportswriters to celebrate the arrival of another "M" star in the Cardinal outfield, following such past heroes as Pepper Martin, Joe Medwick, Terry Moore, and the still-active Stan Musial.

The sharp-eyed Moon, who hit a home run in his first big league at-bat, collected 193 hits, fifth best total in the league, and with those hits he built a .304 batting average.

Moon followed up his fine rookie season with three .290-plus years, then slipped to .238 in 1958, whereupon the Cardinals traded him to the Dodgers. In Los Angeles, Wally quickly regained his batting eye, batting .302, .299, and then a career-high .328 in 1961, before beginning a slow decline that carried him out of the big leagues in 1965.

Of a possible 24 votes, Moon received 17, with Chicago Cubs shortstop Ernie Banks coming in second with four. Milwaukee righthander Gene Conley received two votes; and one lone vote went to another Milwaukee rookie, Henry Aaron, who batted .280 and hit 13 home runs.

Moon's 1954 Record

G	AB	HITS	2B	3B	HR	RUNS	RBI	SB	BAV
151	635	193	29	9	12	106	76	18	.304

Cardinals rookie star Wally Moon who was to have his best seasons with the Los Angeles Dodgers.

Henry Aaron, who received just one vote for Rookie of the Year in 1954.

1955: Bill Virdon

In 1955, for the second year in a row, the St. Louis Cardinals fed a Rookie of the Year outfielder into their lineup. Following Wally Moon in winning freshman distinction was 24-year-old Bill Virdon, who batted .281 and played center field with great skill.

The poker-faced, scholarly-looking Virdon possessed a sharp line-drive bat, though this year he did hit 17 home runs, a career high. The following year he batted his career high, .319, but most of that hitting was done for the Pittsburgh Pirates, to whom he was traded in May. Virdon spent the rest of his playing career with the Pirates, whom he later managed to a pennant in 1972. The former Rookie of the Year also managed the New York Yankees, Houston Astros and Montreal Expos. One of Bill's distinctions is that he was the first manager to be fired by George Steinbrenner (in mid-season, 1975), putting his name at the top of a list that seems to know no end. Bill's departure made room for the first Billy Martin administration in New York.

In winning the Rookie award, Virdon easily beat out a pair of righthanded pitchers—Philadelphia's Jack Meyer and Brooklyn's Don Bessent.

Virdon's 1955 Record

G	AB	HITS	2B	3B	HR	RUNS	RBI	SB	BAV
144	534	150	18	6	17	58	68	2	.281

Bill Virdon

1956: Frank Robinson

One of the great careers in major-league annals was that of Frank Robinson, and he began it in thunderous fashion in 1956. The 20-year-old outfielder joined a Cincinnati Reds club that was noted for its heavy mashers and immediately became one of them. He tied Wally Berger's 1930 rookie record with 38 home runs, while batting .290 and scoring 122 runs. The Reds' 221 home runs that year tied a league record, with five players hitting 25 or more bingo shots: Robinson 38, Wally Post 36, Ted Kluszewski 35, Gus Bell 29, Ed Bailey 28. But they still came in third.

Robinson became the National League's first unanimous choice for Rookie of the Year, winning every one of the 24 possible votes. He was notable for his power hitting, but the opposition, as well as his own teammates, also respected his intensity on the ball field. Kluszewski said of him: "You had to watch him, and not just because he could pound the baseball. He was only twenty years old when he came up, but he played with a seriousness and a purpose that made him seem much older. He wasn't cocky, but I would call him the most self-confident 20-year-old I ever saw."

As he grew older, Robinson's personal qualities matured into those of leadership, and in 1975 he became major-league baseball's first black manager when he was appointed to lead the Cleveland Indians. Robinson the manager proved to be as blunt and direct as Robinson the player had been. When some of his players complained that he was aloof, the skipper said, "I have no trouble communicating. The players just don't like what I have to say." Another player, pointing out that Frank was tough but fair, put it this way: "He'll step on your feet, but he won't mess up your shoe shine."

Robinson's 1956 Record

G	AB	HITS	2B	3B	HR	RUNS	RBI	SB	BAV
152	572	166	27	6	38	122	83	8	.290

Frank Robinson—from Rookie of the Year to the Hall of Fame.

1957: Jack Sanford

The Philadelphia Phillies' Jack Sanford was a rookie in name only in 1957. Turning 27-years-old as the season got underway, Sanford had been in professional baseball since 1948. For nine years he had been working his way toward daylight, making all the ports of call in the Philadelphia farm system: Bradford, New York; Dover, Delaware; Americus, Georgia; Wilmington, Delaware; Schenectady, New York; Baltimore and then Syracuse, before some final seasoning in the military.

So it was a highly-primed Jack Sanford who joined the Phillies in the spring of 1957.

"We knew he had good stuff," Phillies manager Mayo Smith said. "I figured he'd be all right, but he was better than that and really surprised everybody."

By the end of the season, Sanford was the ace of a staff that included Robin Roberts and Curt Simmons. The hard-throwing righthander compiled a 19-8 record and led the league with 188 strikeouts. He was easily the league's Rookie of the Year, beating out teammate Ed Bouchee, a first base-man who batted .293 and Cubs righthander Dick Drott, a 15-game winner who fanned 170.

Sanford pitched in the big leagues for four different teams, until 1967. His top year was 1962, when he was 24-7 for the San Francisco Giants.

Sanford's 1957 Record

WON	LOST	PCT.	G	GS	CG	INP	HITS	BB	SO	SH	ERA
19	8	.704	33	33	15	236	194	94	188	3	3.08

Philadelphia Phillies fastballer Jack Sanford.

1958:
Orlando Cepeda

When the New York Giants moved to San Francisco in 1958, they brought along with them the man generally acknowledged as baseball's premier player, Willie Mays. The independent-minded San Franciscans, however, decided to heap their adoration not on Willie but on a 20-year-old rookie firstbaseman named Orlando Cepeda. It was as if the Giant fans wanted a brand-new, morning-fresh hero and not one tainted by the adulation of the East Coast.

Cepeda won the hearts of the fans quickly and emphatically. Possessor of a physique that earned him the nickname, "Baby Bull," the powerful youngster made a smashing debut, batting .312, hitting 25 home runs, driving in 96 runs, and leading the league with 38 doubles.

A few other talented rookies broke into the league that year, including Cepeda's Giant teammates Jim Davenport (third base) and Willie Kirkland (outfield) and the Cardinals' young center fielder Curt Flood. But as far as the writers were concerned, there was only one—Cepeda was Rookie of the Year by unanimous vote.

In 1967, Cepeda also won the league's MVP Award. He is one of eight former Rookies of the Year to go on to take the big award.

Cepeda's 1958 Record

G	AB	HITS	2B	3B	HR	RUNS	RBI	SB	BAV
148	603	188	38	4	25	88	96	15	.312

Orlando Cepeda, a unanimous Rookie of the Year selection in 1958.

1959:
Willie McCovey

For the third time in four years, the National League Rookie of the Year was a unanimous selection, and for the second year in a row, he was a member of the San Francisco Giants. He was a tall, loose-jointed 21-year-old firstbaseman named Willie McCovey. The Alabama-bred youngster had a sweeping lefthanded swing that was admired as much for its purity as for its power.

Nicknamed "Stretch" for his 6'4" seemingly boneless frame, McCovey broke into just 52 games (he joined the club in the beginning of August), but made so deep an impression that he swept the Rookie of the Year vote.

In his first major-league game, Willie had performed like a future Rookie of the Year, like a future home run and RBI champ, like a future Hall of Famer, like a man who in his prime was the most feared hitter in the league. He had faced the great Robin Roberts and had hit two singles and two triples, each hit going, as one writer said, "like a rifle shot."

How feared was McCovey? Well, in 1969, he received 45 intentional bases on balls, by far the major league record. That big, symmetrical rip he took at home plate at times looked broad enough to decapitate the third baseman.

Having both McCovey and Orlando Cepeda on the club presented a problem for the Giants. Both were young, hard-hitting firstbasemen, and neither possessed the defensive skills for any other position.

Wanting to keep both of their heavy gunners, the Giants wrestled with the problem for years, trying first Cepeda in the outfield and then McCovey. It wasn't until 1966 that the club finally resolved things—they traded Cepeda to the Cardinals.

McCovey's 1959 Record

G	AB	HITS	2B	3B	HR	RUNS	RBI	SB	BAV
52	192	68	9	5	13	32	38	2	.354

The most feared hitter of his time—Willie McCovey.

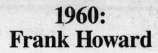

1960:
Frank Howard

At 6'7" and an estimated 270 pounds, Frank Howard was a natural for nicknames—"Hondo," "The Monster," "Gulliver in a baseball suit," etc. The nicknames were always delivered with smiles and perhaps a gentle pat on the back, since it is not unlikely that Howard was the strongest man ever to play in the big leagues. Fortunately for those around him, he was also a gentle man, with a balanced disposition.

"When a fight broke out on the field," Dodger manager Walter Alston said, "the safest place to be was standing next to Howard. Nobody would go near him. Frank was the great peacemaker out there. Once we had a brawl somewhere and two guys had each other in headlocks. They were so tangled up it looked like they'd need a locksmith to get them apart. Frank headed over toward them and they saw him and broke apart and scattered."

Frank Howard's aggressions came out at home plate. Twice he was the American League's home run champion while playing for the Washington Senators. Throughout his playing career (which ended in 1973), he hit 382 home runs, many of them for breathtaking distance.

In 1958, the Ohio State product received a $108,000 bonus to sign with the Dodgers. The 23-year-old slugger joined the Dodgers in 1960, batted .268, hit 23 home runs for the power-poor club and was voted Rookie of the Year. It was not a vintage year for rookies in the National League—the runner-ups were first baseman Pancho Herrera and pitcher Art Mahaffey of the Phillies. The National League rookie who was to have the most distinguished career was Cubs third-baseman Ron Santo, but he broke in quietly (.251, nine home runs) and attracted just one vote.

Howard's strike zone was so big, one writer said, that it should have been "subdivided." Inevitably, Howard was always the most prominent man on a ball field.

"His size made him noticeable," Alston said, "and his power made him scary. A man that size standing up there with a bat in his hand scared the hell out of a lot of pitchers. Some of them felt that he was big enough to go up to the plate without a bat."

Willie Mays was a player with a flair for the dramatic—clutch hits, exciting baserunning, and theatrical plays in the outfield. One day in Pittsburgh he did something in center field no one had ever seen before—unable to get his glove far enough across his body to grab a hooking line drive, he reached out and caught the ball with his bare hand.

Racing in after the inning, Willie was expecting plaudits from his teammates. By the orders of manager Leo Durocher, however, the dugout remained quiet. Puzzled, Willie looked around. No one said anything. Finally, Mays said to Durocher, "Leo, didn't you see what I did out there?"

"No," Leo said. "And you're going to have to do it again before I believe it."

Howard's 1960 Record

G	AB	HITS	2B	3B	HR	RUNS	RBI	SB	BAV
117	448	120	15	2	23	54	77	0	.268

Frank Howard, fortress-sized slugger of the Los Angeles Dodgers.

1961:
Billy Williams

As of the 1987 season, the Chicago Cubs had just two players voted Rookie of the Year, and they came back-to-back in 1961 and 1962. Outfielder Billy Williams, the 1961 selection, went on to become one of the most admired and consistent hitters of his era, putting together a long career that ended in 1976 and culminated with his election to the Hall of Fame.

Consistency can make some men dull and small-minded. In a baseball player, however, it is a prized virtue, especially when it is maintained at the levels achieved by Williams. For 13 straight years, he never hit fewer than 21 home runs, drove in less than 84 runs, or batted under .276. Underlining this consistency was the National League record he established for consecutive games played, 1,117 (since broken by Steve Garvey).

Williams broke in with the Cubs in 1961, hitting the way he was going to hit for the next dozen years—.278 batting average, 25 home runs, 86 runs batted in. In winning the Rookie of the Year award, Billy beat out Milwaukee's young catcher Joe Torre, who also batted .278 but didn't post the power stats that Williams did. The only other newcomer to draw a vote was Billy's teammate, lefthander John Curtis.

For years, Williams was part of a feared slugging trio in the middle of the Cubs' lineup, along with Ron Santo and Ernie Banks. Each had long and resoundingly productive careers; and each retired with the same lament—never having played in a World Series.

Banks always had a reputation for cheerfulness, while

Williams was known as the quiet man. This led Cubs right-hander Ferguson Jenkins, apparently in a somewhat disgruntled mood, to remark: "I don't think those people at Wrigley Field ever saw but two players they liked. Ernie Banks and Billy Williams. Billy never said anything and Ernie always said the right thing."

Williams' 1961 Record

G	AB	HITS	2B	3B	HR	RUNS	RBI	SB	BAV
146	529	147	20	7	25	75	86	6	.278

Billy Williams, who began the journey to the Hall of Fame as 1961's National League Rookie of the Year.

1962: Ken Hubbs

On the morning of February 13, 1964, a white Cessna 172 took off from Provo Airport in Provo, Utah, on a 550-mile flight to Morrow Airport, near Colton, California. The temperature was below zero, there were snow flurries, visibility was less than four miles. It had been suggested to the pilot and passenger that perhaps it might be best to postpone their flight and wait for more favorable flying conditions. But the 22-year-old pilot and his 23-year-old friend decided to go, hoping to fly into better weather.

Not many moments after takeoff, the Cessna quickly lost altitude and plunged through the ice of Utah Lake. Two days later, the bodies of Ken Hubbs, the pilot (his pilot's license was just three weeks old) and a boyhood chum were pulled from the lake.

Ken Hubbs had completed his second season as Chicago Cubs second baseman in 1963 and was just a few weeks away from joining the club for spring training.

At the age of 20, the quiet, serious-minded Hubbs had broken in at second base for the Cubs, turned in a fine year and been voted the National League's Rookie of the Year. A singles hitter, Ken rapped 172 hits and batted .260, his performance marred only by a league-high 129 strikeouts.

While his hitting was acceptable, it was in the field that the youngster truly starred. Beginning on June 13, he began setting new standards for defensive perfection at second base playing 78 consecutive errorless games, during which he handled 418 chances without mishap. Hubbs easily broke Red Schoendienst's old National League record of 57 straight errorless games and just barely broke Bobby Doerr's major league mark of 73 games and 414 chances. (Hubbs' record has since been bettered by several second-basemen in both leagues.)

In winning Rookie of the Year honors, Hubbs enjoyed almost a clean sweep, with one vote going to Pittsburgh first-baseman Donn Clendenon.

Ken's batting average dipped to .235 in his sophomore year and he had resolved to do better in 1964, but he was never to get the chance.

Hubbs' 1962 Record

B	AB	HITS	2B	3B	HR	RUNS	RBI	SB	BAV
160	661	172	24	9	5	90	49	3	.260

Ken Hubbs, who had a tragically short career.

1963: Pete Rose

The Big Red Machine revved up to full gear in the mid-1970's, and by the time it stopped blazing up and down the byways of the National League, it had been acclaimed as one of the most illustrious baseball units of all time. Cincinnati had begun building the machine in 1963, installing a sparkplug named Pete Rose.

A 22-year-old secondbaseman, Pete joined his hometown club with the reputation for being a nonstop hustler (he had raced out 30 triples one year in the minors) and for the next 23 years did nothing to dispel it.

This was a fellow who embraced the game of baseball heart and soul, virtually to the exclusion of everything else. "I'd walk through hell in a gasoline suit to keep playing baseball," was one of his better-known quotes. A friend told this one about Pete: "In high school, his history teacher asked the class to list the nine greatest Americans, but Rose could only come up with eight. His explanation was, 'I couldn't think of a thirdbaseman.'"

Coming up as a secondbaseman, in time he became an All-Star at that position as well as at third base, first base, right field and left field. Although primarily a singles and doubles hitter, his low crouching appearance at home plate became as crowd-pleasing as the stance of the most powerful home-run hitter. In time, he became the most prolific collector of base hits in baseball history, passing the 3,000 mark, then 4,000, then Ty Cobb's all-time record of 4,191.

He finally retired with an unequalled 4,256 hits, one of those baseball records that have high walls and a moat around them.

It all started in 1963, with a Rookie of the Year performance by the intense young switch-hitter. Pete batted .273 and racked up 170 hits and scored 101 runs, the first of ten times he was to reach the century mark in runs scored.

Pete was almost a sweep in the voting, drawing 17 of a possible 20 votes; Mets second baseman Ron Hunt, a Rose-type of player, received two votes and the Phillies' righthander Ray Culp, a 14-game winner, pulled the remaining vote.

Rose never formally announced his retirement as a player, but rather just faded away. He took his last swings in August, 1986, by which time he was manager of the Cincinnati Reds. For his epitaph, baseball's number one accumulator of base hits suggested this:

"Here lies the man who could hit forever."

When Pete Rose joined the Reds for his rookie year in the spring of 1963, his frenetic, nonstop hustle quickly caught everyone's attention. Even a base on balls sent Pete out of the batter's box at full speed. Finally one writer said, "The way that kid takes off down the line, you'd think first base was located down in the right-field corner."

Rose's 1963 Record

G	AB	HITS	2B	3B	HR	RUNS	RBI	SB	BAV
157	623	170	25	9	6	101	41	13	.273

Pete Rose, once upon a time.

1964: Dick Allen

Controversial and talented: these will probably remain the indelible words on Dick Allen's dossier. He had likes and dislikes, virtues and shortcomings. He liked horses and he disliked spring training, batting practice, and showing up at the ball park at the appointed hour. He also disliked artificial playing surfaces, saying that if a horse couldn't eat it, then he didn't want to play on it. As far as spring training and batting practice are concerned, he probably really didn't need them, at least, not when he was young (young being, in some cases, a mental as well as a physical age).

Some of his managers allowed themselves to be distressed by Allen's casual habits; others simply let him do it his way and play ball. Really, there wasn't very much you could do with him. If you lectured him, he listened, then went out and did whatever he wanted to do. If you fined him, he paid, and then went right on doing whatever it was that he shouldn't have been doing in the first place. If you asked the front office for some help, you might find that they were unwilling to offend your star. (No one, however, ever questioned Allen's abilities or his hustle on the field. Getting him out there on time was the problem.) His teammates, with whom he was generally quite popular, were in awe of his talent.

The Philadelphia Phillies' Rookie of the Year in 1964 (he was known as "Richie" then) was a thirdbaseman who packed explosive power, hitting 29 home runs, leading the league with 13 triples, and batting .318. A free-swinger, he struck out 138 times, the most in the league. The 22-year-old slugger ("He hits them over buildings," Mets manager

41

Casey Stengel said) played in 162 games in 1964, tying a record for rookies.

Allen's freshman season was the year the Phillies went into the final weeks of the schedule with a 6¹/₂ game lead and then blew a pennant they apparently had securely in hand.

In being voted Rookie of the Year, Allen was almost a unanimous choice, pulling 18 of 20 votes. Dividing the other two votes were a pair of rookies quite impressive in their own right—Milwaukee's Rico Carty, who batted .330, and San Francisco's Jim Hart, who hit 31 home runs.

Allen played in the big leagues for 15 years, appearing with five different clubs (in 1972 he was American League MVP while playing for the White Sox). He retired in 1977 with 351 home runs and a .292 lifetime batting average.

Allen had a rationale for his restrained approach to calisthenics, batting practice and punctuality.

"Your body is like a bar of soap," he said. "It gradually wears down from repeated use."

Allen's 1964 Record

G	AB	HITS	2B	3B	HR	RUNS	RBI	SB	BAV
162	632	201	38	13	29	125	91	3	.318

Dick Allen—they called him Richie then.

Dick Allen

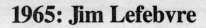

1965: Jim Lefebvre

As of the 1987 season, the Dodgers (in Brooklyn and Los Angeles) had more Rookies of the Year than any other team in the major leagues—11. Number six on this list was switch-hitting second-baseman Jim Lefebvre, a 22-year-old Californian. Jim was the popular choice for rookie honors, winning 13 of 20 votes. Coming in second was another secondbaseman, destined to turn in one of the most blazingly successful careers in baseball history—Houston's Joe Morgan, who received four votes. San Francisco reliever Frank Linzy had the remaining three votes.

Lefebvre was a member of one of the most unique infields ever in baseball as all four regulars were switch-hitters: firstbaseman Wes Parker, secondbaseman, Lefebvre, shortstop Maury Wills, and thirdbaseman Jim Gilliam.

"Having all those switch-hitters in the lineup helped immeasurably that year," Dodger manager Walter Alston said. "You see, we were a bit light on offense."

"A bit light" was putting it modestly—the Dodgers were out-hit by six other teams in the ten-team league, out-scored by seven teams, and out-homered by everybody. Nevertheless, they went on to win the pennant and World Series, doing it primarily on the arms of Sandy Koufax (26-8) and Don Drysdale (23-12), whose win totals should be kept in mind whenever one hears of some pitcher blaming his record on lack of support.

Like the rest of his teammates, Lefebvre didn't frighten any infielders or damage any fences with his hitting. Nevertheless, he was one of the team's big "power" hitters—his 12 home runs tied outfielder Lou Johnson for the team lead, and his 69 runs batted in were one short of the Dodger high that year. Indeed, the Dodger "offense" was led by Wills' 94 stolen bases.

"'One game at a time' is a common phrase in baseball," Alston said. "Well, for us that year it was 'one base at a time.' We just kept on doing it all season, and when it was over we'd won 97 games and the pennant."

Lefebvre's 1965 Record

G	AB	HITS	2B	3B	HR	RUNS	RBI	SB	BAV
157	544	136	21	4	12	57	69	3	.250

Jim Lefevbre, switch-hitting second baseman of the Dodgers.

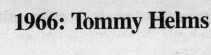

1966: Tommy Helms

Six National League rookies pulled votes for the top of the class in 1966, with Cincinnati's Tommy Helms receiving 12, while the five other players divided the remaining eight votes.

The 25-year-old Helms, a thirdbaseman, was quite an experienced player by the time he finally made the majors, having spent seven years in the Cincinnati organization. Tommy was joining a team that was gradually shaping its "Big Red Machine," the most bruising baseball outfit of the 1970's, with Tony Perez and Pete Rose already in place. Helms, however, was not going to be part of it—the Reds were going to trade him to Houston after the 1971 season in a deal that would bring Joe Morgan to Cincinnati. Tommy did play on Cincinnati's 1970 pennant winners as a secondbaseman. The versatile Helms was equally comfortable at second, short and third.

The 1966 Rookie of the Year batted .284 and showed a good eye at home plate, striking out just 31 times in 542 official plate appearances.

Following Helms with just three votes was Houston shortstop Sonny Jackson, who batted .292 and stole 49 bases (his league-leading 37 errors may have cost him the rookie award). Getting two votes was San Francisco infielder Tito Fuentes, while Chicago catcher Randy Hundley, Mets outfielder Cleon Jones, and St. Louis lefthander Larry Jaster got one apiece.

Helm's 1966 Record

G	AB	HITS	2B	3B	HR	RUNS	RBI	SB	BAV
138	542	154	23	1	9	72	49	3	.284

Cincinnati's Tommy Helms.

1967: Tom Seaver

The man described as "the greatest right-hander to pitch in New York since Christy Mathewson" broke in with the New York Mets in 1967 and remained in the big leagues until 1986. On the mound, Tom Seaver was both a power pitcher and an artisan: he was also highly intelligent, shrewdly analytical and self-disciplined. He was nicknamed, among other things, "The Franchise," and it was most appropriate, for when he joined the Mets in 1967, their brief history was one of losing, struggling, and buffoonery. He quickly gave them class, style, distinction and credibility. Not since Babe Ruth joined the Yankees in 1920 had a player injected so life-giving a presence into a team.

The boyishly handsome Seaver had pitched just one year of minor league ball when he joined the Mets in spring training in 1967. The 22-year-old righthander impressed everyone with his maturity on the mound, his insights into his profession, and, most importantly, with his blazing knee-high fastball and the control he had over it. A few years later, after Seaver had helped pitch the Mets to the pennant with a 25-7 record, someone asked manager Gil Hodges if he had ever seen a young pitcher with a better combination of poise, stuff and know-how. "No," Gil said. "Nor an older pitcher either."

The club Seaver joined in 1967 had finished ninth the year before. In his rookie year they finished tenth, losing 101 games. But this was hardly the fault of the young Californian: in breaking the seal on his big league career, Seaver was 16-13, with a 2.76 ERA (that ERA would remain under 3.00 for 11 of his first 12 years in the bigs). He had 170 strikeouts; for the next nine consecutive seasons, he would have over 200 strikeouts, one of the many major-league records he established. When he retired, he had a lifetime record of 311-205 and was third on the all-time strikeout list, with 3,640.

In an interview given early in his career, Seaver, stressing that dreams and ambition without hard work were meaningless, said, "Because there isn't much time for a ballplayer, he has to realize when he's young that he has to work to get where he wants to go."

In winning Rookie of the Year honors, Seaver outpolled two other pitchers who also enjoyed productive freshman seasons—St. Louis Cardinals righthander Dick Hughes, who was 16-6 and helped pitch the Cardinals to the pennant (a sore arm aborted Hughes' career a year later), and Cincinnati Reds righthander Gary Nolan, who was 14-8 and had 206 strikeouts.

Seaver's 1967 Record

WON	LOST	PCT.	G	GS	CG	INP	HITS	BB	SO	SH	ERA
16	13	.552	35	34	18	251	224	78	170	2	2.76

Tom Seaver, who went from star rookie to 300-game winner.

1968: Johnny Bench

In two successive years, 1967 and 1968, the National League introduced a pair of rookies who were to become two of the most dominant forces in baseball history—Tom Seaver in 1967, and in 1968 Johnny Bench, the 20-year-old catcher for the Cincinnati Reds.

Bench was the first catcher ever to be selected as the National League's Rookie of the Year. To all who saw the young Oklahoman breaking in, it was apparent that here was a superstar in embryo. When the young man asked Ted Williams to autograph a baseball for him, Williams signed it to "Johnny Bench—a sure Hall of Famer."

Williams' eye for talent was never sharper. Catching 154 games for the Reds at the age of 20, Bench impressed people with his maturity behind the plate, his acumen at handling pitchers, his defensive skills, and his powerful throwing arm, which soon became one of baseball's most intimidating forces.

"He was so good behind the plate," Mets manager Gil Hodges said, "that sometimes you forgot what a strong hitter he was."

Bench not only hit for a respectable average (.267 life-time), but with exceptional power (twice leading the league with 40 or more home runs). In 1968, the National League's Rookie of the Year batted .275 and hit 15 home runs, while leading league catchers in putouts and assists.

When Bench joined the Reds that year, two of the major dynamos of what would become "The Big Red Machine" were already whirring, Tony Perez and Pete Rose. They would later be joined by George Foster, Joe

Morgan, Ken Griffey and Dave Concepcion. With Bench anchoring behind the plate, they would go on to win six division titles, four pennants, and back-to-back World Series in 1975 and 1976.

Despite his obvious brilliance, Bench's rookie award was a close thing—he won by a single point over the Mets' young southpaw Jerry Koosman, who was 19-12 for a ninth-place club.

Jerry Koosman, who narrowly lost the Rookie of the Year Award to Johnny Bench in 1968.

The career that began so auspiciously for Johnny Bench in 1968 would culminate with many people calling him the greatest catcher in baseball history. The previous candidates for catcher on the all-time team were Bill Dickey and Mickey Cochrane, a pair of 1930s heroes between whom the most knowledgeable baseball people found it hard to decide.

Johnny Bench.

Now when the deep thinkers try to choose between Dickey and Cochrane, it's quite possible they are selecting the second-greatest catcher of them all, thanks to Johnny Bench, whose career was in neon lights from his rookie year until his retirement in 1983.

Bench's 1968 Record

G	AB	HITS	2B	3B	HR	RUNS	RBI	SB	BAV
154	564	155	40	2	15	67	82	1	.275

Johnny Bench in a tough confrontation at home plate. Note that the runner, Al Oliver, has knocked the ball free.

1969: Ted Sizemore

By 1969, injuries had reduced the Los Angeles Dodgers' 1965 Rookie of the Year secondbaseman Jim Lefebvre to part-time status. Undeterred, the Dodgers reached down into their ever-productive farm system and came up with another Rookie of the Year secondbaseman, 24-year-old Ted Sizemore.

In 1965, the Dodgers had presented an all-switch-hitting infield in Wes Parker, Lefebvre, Maury Wills and Jim Gilliam. In 1969, the righthanded-hitting Sizemore was the only non-switcher in an infield that still included Parker at first base and Wills at shortstop, with Bill Sudakis at third base.

In this first year of divisional play (the National League had expanded to 12 teams with the addition of San Diego in the newly formed Western Division and Montreal in the Eastern), the Dodgers came in fourth. So the new man was one of the bright spots, breaking in with a .271 batting average and showing a snappy glove in the field (he also gave the Dodgers 46 games at shortstop during the year).

Sizemore captured 14 of the possible 24 votes for outstanding rookie. Coming in second with three votes apiece were Montreal's thirdbaseman, Coco Laboy, and Pittsburgh's first baseman-outfielder, Al Oliver, who was to become one of the most consistent .300 hitters in the game. Pulling two votes each were Atlanta catcher Bob Didier and Philadelphia outfielder Larry Hisle, who later became a star slugger in the American League.

In 1970, Sizemore improved his batting average to .306. Nevertheless, the power-starved Dodgers traded him to the Cardinals for another former Rookie of the Year, Dick Allen. Sizemore returned to the Dodgers in 1976 and later played for the Phillies and Cubs, before ending his career with the Boston Red Sox in 1980.

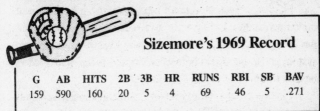

Sizemore's 1969 Record

G	AB	HITS	2B	3B	HR	RUNS	RBI	SB	BAV
159	590	160	20	5	4	69	46	5	.271

Ted Sizemore, one of the many Dodger Rookies of the Year.

1970: Carl Morton

The newly-formed Montreal Expos were in just the second year of their big league existence when they came up with a Rookie of the Year. He was Carl Morton, a 26-year-old righthander who surprised everybody by posting an 18-11 record for a Montreal club that finished last in the Eastern Division.

In 1964, Morton had received a $60,000 bonus to sign with the Milwaukee Braves. Originally an outfielder, he switched to the mound in 1967, while he was playing for Kinston in the Carolina League. When the Montreal club was formed in the fall of 1968, the Expos drafted Morton from the Braves' (now located in Atlanta) roster. After one more year of seasoning, he joined the Expos in 1970 and delivered his fine rookie season, which turned out to be the best of his eight-year big league career, during which he was 87-92.

Morton's bugaboo in his rookie year was wildness—he led the league with 125 bases on balls, though he tempered this with 154 strikeouts. His four shutouts tied him for second-best in the league.

Morton pulled 11 votes for outstanding rookie, outpolling by three votes Cincinnati outfielder Bernie Carbo, who broke in with a .310 average and 21 home runs. Philadelphia shortstop Larry Bowa, with a long career ahead of him, received three votes. Cincinnati righthander Wayne Simpson and Houston outfielder Cesar Cedeno each received a single vote. Simpson may well have won the rookie award had not his year been foreshortened by a mid-season arm injury, holding him to a 14-3 record.

Most of those who followed Morton in the voting were

to have longer careers—Carbo, Bowa and Cedeno. Carl was traded to Atlanta in 1973, where he had three successful years, winning 15, 16, and 17, then slumping to 4-9 in 1976, when he left the big leagues.

Morton's 1970 Record

WON	LOST	PCT.	G	GS	CG	INP	HITS	BB	SO	SH	ERA
18	11	.621	43	37	10	285	281	125	154	4	3.60

Montreal's ace righthander, Carl Morton.

1971: Earl Williams

Going into the 1971 season, there was no shortage of first-rate catchers in the National League. Pittsburgh had Manny Sanguillen; St. Louis, Ted Simmons; New York, Jerry Grote; Philadelphia, Tim McCarver; San Francisco, Dick Dietz; and Cincinnati had Johnny Bench. In 1971 Atlanta's rookie Earl Williams was added to this list. He was the second catcher to be voted National League Rookie of the Year (Bench was the first).

Interestingly, the big, strong 23-year-old Williams didn't become a catcher until he reached the major leagues, having played infield and outfield in the minors. Liking Earl's bat and needing a righthanded swinger behind the plate, the Braves put him there for 72 games (he divided the rest of the time between third base and first base).

Williams could hit—he poled 33 home runs during his first major-league season and drove in 87 runs, batting .260. The Braves were congratulating themselves on having discovered a companion slugger for the aging Henry Aaron. The following year, Williams hit 28 homers and again drove in 87 runs. After the season, however, the Braves traded Williams to Baltimore in a deal that brought righthander Pat Dobson to Atlanta.

Williams played in Baltimore, then Atlanta again, followed by Montreal, and finally Oakland. He retired in 1977 without ever having fulfilled the high promise of his rookie season.

Only two rookies pulled votes for the yearly award in the National League in 1971, Williams and Phillies outfielder Willie Montanez. The latter hit 30 home runs, drove in 99 runs, and batted .255, as he launched a 14-year major-league career that saw him rotate through the rosters of nine different teams.

Williams' 1971 Record

G	AB	HITS	2B	3B	HR	RUNS	RBI	SB	BAV
145	497	129	14	1	33	64	87	0	.260

Atlanta catcher, Earl Williams, who never quite lived up to his early success.

1972: Jon Matlack

In 1967, the New York Mets produced the National League's Rookie of the Year—righthander Tom Seaver. In 1968, they just missed making it two in a row, when Johnny Bench edged out lefthander Jerry Koosman for rookie honors by one vote. Four years later, another Mets pitcher stood out among the freshman crop, and this time the Rookie of the Year voting wasn't even close.

The new man was 22-year-old lefthander Jon Matlack, of whom one teammate said, "He has so much stuff, it's scary." In 1972, the hard-throwing Matlack showed that stuff to good advantage, winning 15, losing 10, firing four shutouts and logging the fourth-best earned-run average in the league, 2.32.

Matlack drew most of the Rookie of the Year votes, getting 19. Four went to San Francisco Giants catcher Dave Rader. Matlack's Mets teammate John Milner received one vote.

Matlack was part of an extraordinary line of young pitchers developed by the Mets organization. This included Nolan Ryan, Tom Seaver, Jerry Koosman, Tug McGraw, Jeff Reardon, Mike Scott, Dwight Gooden, Ron Darling, Roger McDowell, Randy Myers, and others; some of whom, like Reardon and Scott, have done their best work for other teams.

The 1972 Rookie of the Year proved to be the real thing, following his successful break-in season with four more years of strong pitching for the Mets. In 1973, he joined with Seaver and Koosman to pitch the Mets to the team's second pennant. Matlack led the league in shutouts in 1974 and again in 1976 (his 17 wins that year were his best big league total).

After a dip to 7-15 in 1977, Matlack was dealt away, landing with the Texas Rangers, for whom he had one strong year before slowly losing his effectiveness. His last big league season was 1983.

Matlack's 1972 Record

WON	LOST	PCT.	G	GS	CG	INP	HITS	BB	SO	SH	ERA
15	10	.600	34	32	8	244	215	71	169	4	2.32

New York Mets lefty, Jon Matlack, who teamed with Tom Seaver and Jerry Koosman to pitch the Mets to the 1973 pennant.

1973: Gary Matthews

Nine National League rookies pulled votes for top honors in 1973, more than ever before; and among them were some highly gifted players with long, productive careers ahead of them. Leading the way, and an easy winner with 11 of the 24 votes, was San Francisco Giants outfielder Gary Matthews, who broke in with a .300 batting average. With Matthews in left, Garry Maddox in center, and Bobby Bonds in right, the Giants had one of the most talented young outfields in baseball. But as was the Giants' habit in those days, all three were gone within a few years. (They had already traded George Foster two years before.)

The Giants lost Matthews to free agency after the 1976 season, traded Maddox in May 1975, to the Phillies for Willie Montanez, and in October 1974, traded Bonds to the Yankees for Bobby Murcer.

The 1973 Rookie of the Year played in the majors for 16 years, putting in time with the Giants, Braves, Phillies, Cubs, and finally the Seattle Mariners, retiring in 1987 with a lifetime .281 batting average. Reunited with Maddox in the Phillies' outfield in 1981, the two ex-Giants helped the team to the National League pennant in 1983.

Finishing second in the 1973 rookie balloting was Montreal righthander Steve Rodgers, who broke in with a 10-5 record and a shiny 1.54 ERA. Steve drew 3½ votes (one writer split his ballot).

Getting two votes apiece were Phillies catcher Bob Boone, Giants righthanded reliever Elias Sosa, and Cincinnati thirdbaseman Dan Driessen. Boone was to go on, and on and on, catching for the Phillies and then the California Angels, until he had set a new major league record for games caught.

Pulling one vote apiece were San Diego outfielder Johnny Grubb (a .311 hitter) and a pair of Dodger infielders: thirdbaseman Ron Cey and secondbaseman Davey Lopes. Cey and Lopes became part of the longest-lasting infield unit in baseball history—7½ years—when they teamed up with shortstop Bill Russell and firstbaseman Steve Garvey.

The remaining half vote went to another player who broke in impressively (.324) and was to have a most productive big league career—Pittsburgh outfielder Richie Zisk. Zisk teamed with Al Oliver and Willie Stargell to give the Pirates a real "lumber-company outfield." And sitting on the bench for the Pirates was still another rookie outfielder, Dave Parker, who got into just 54 games.

Overall, it was a most impressive rookie group that entered the National League in 1973.

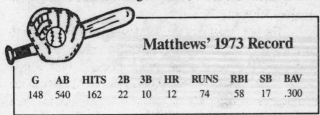

Matthews' 1973 Record

G	AB	HITS	2B	3B	HR	RUNS	RBI	SB	BAV
148	540	162	22	10	12	74	58	17	.300

San Francisco's Gary Matthews.

1974: Bake McBride

The St. Louis Cardinals had not had a Rookie of the Year since Wally Moon and Bill Virdon won back-to-back awards in 1954 and 1955. The drought was broken in 1974 by 25-year-old outfielder Arnold Ray "Bake" McBride.

The lefthanded-hitter's .309 batting average was no fluke—he would hit over .300 for each of his first four years in the big leagues and wind up with a .299 average for his 11-year career.

McBride, who showed some flash on the bases with 30 steals, was part of a .300-hitting Cardinal outfield, joining Reggie Smith (.309) and Lou Brock (.306). They drove the Cardinals to within 1½ games of the Eastern Division title.

McBride's .300 bat seemed to assure him a long career in the Cardinal outfield, but then in June 1977 he was traded to the Phillies. There he helped the club to division titles in 1977, 1978 and 1980, plus a pennant in the last year. He finished up his career with Cleveland in 1983, just 33-years-old.

Bake was an easy winner in the rookie voting, polling 16 votes to seven for Houston's Gregg Gross (who batted .314) and just one for Chicago third baseman Bill Madlock, a future four-time batting champion and .313 hitter (in 1974).

McBride's 1974 Record

G	AB	HITS	2B	3B	HR	RUNS	RBI	SB	BAV
150	559	173	19	5	6	81	56	30	.309

Bake McBride, the Cardinals' .300-hitting young outfielder.

68

1975: John Montefusco

The Rookie of the Year for the National League in 1975 was a colorful, hard-throwing 25-year-old righthander named John Montefusco. The San Francisco Giants brought him up at the tail end of the 1974 season and then promoted him for keeps in 1975. In his first official major league at-bat, Montefusco (known as "the Count") belted a home run. He soon hit a second home run, but if the Giants thought they had brought up a hitting pitcher, well, John went 7-for-80 the next year, batting .088.

Fortunately for the Count, he didn't have to depend on his bat for a living. On the mound he did just fine, and never better than in his first two seasons. The 1975 National League Rookie of the Year posted a handsome 15-9 record, including four shutouts. Along the way he fanned 215 batters, second in the league to Tom Seaver's 243.

Montefusco was a gregarious, likable young man. Exceedingly confident on the mound, he talked a good game and generally was able to back it up. He backed it up even further in 1976 with a 16-14 record that included a September 29 no-hitter against the Atlanta Braves.

The Count, however, never scored the big 20-game season promised by his early success. With a career plagued by injury, Montefusco was one of a group of strong-armed young Giant pitchers who started off with a bang, but failed to fulfill expectations. (The others were lefthander Pete Falcone and righties Ed Halicki and John D'Acquisto.)

After leaving the Giants in 1980, Montefusco pitched for the Atlanta Braves, San Diego Padres, and finally the New York Yankees, retiring with assorted injuries in 1986.

Montefusco won 12 votes for Rookie of the Year, followed by Montreal's Gary Carter (more an outfielder than catcher then), who had nine. Pulling one vote apiece were Montreal third baseman Larry Parrish, Chicago second baseman Manny Trillo, and Cincinnati reliever Rawley Eastwick.

Montefusco's 1975 Record

WON	LOST	PCT.	G	GS	CG	INP	HITS	BB	SO	SH	ERA
15	9	.625	35	34	10	244	210	86	215	4	2.88

The colorful and hard-throwing John Montefusco.

1976: Pat Zachry
Butch Metzger

The voting for the National League's Rookie of the Year in 1976 resulted in a tie between two 24-year-old righthanders, San Diego reliever Butch Metzger and Cincinnati's Pat Zachry. It remains the only tie vote ever for the rookie award in either league.

The tall (6'5"), gaunt Zachry (announcer Vin Scully once said of him, "He looks like he got here on a raft") had spent six years in the Cincinnati organization, pitching steady if unspectacular minor-league ball until being promoted to the big team in 1976. As a member of "The Big Red Machine," one of the most thunderous ball clubs of all time, the rookie turned in a 14-7 record—second-most wins on the staff—and a 2.74 ERA, best on the staff.

Zachry only pitched for the Reds for a year and half. The following June he went to the Mets in the controversial trade that brought Tom Seaver to Cincinnati. Pat's prime years found him buried in a Mets club that finished last or next-to-last for five straight years. In 1983, he was liberated in a trade with the Dodgers and finished up his big-league career with the Phillies in 1985.

Zachry's co-winner, Clarence "Butch" Metzger, had been up briefly with the Giants in 1974 and the Padres in 1975, before joining the Padres in 1976 and becoming their bullpen ace. Like Zachry, Butch had served a long minor-league apprenticeship—seven years—before graduating to the big time.

Metzger's splendid rookie year, which he turned in for a last-place team, saw him tying the major-league record for most consecutive wins by a freshman reliever (10) and establishing another record (since broken) for most appearances by a rookie pitcher (77).

Metzger, however, was to suffer the occupational hazard of many frequently-used relief pitchers—early burnout. Butch was, in fact, a classic example. After going 11-4, with 16 saves, in his rookie year, he found himself traded to the Cardinals the following May. He appeared in 75 games that year, posting a 4-2 record, with seven saves. In the spring of 1978, he was waived to the New York Mets, for whom he pitched ineffectively until sent back to the minors in July. He never returned to the majors.

The only other rookie to receive any votes in 1976 was Cardinal third baseman Heity Cruz, a .228 hitter who drew two votes.

Zachry's 1976 Record

WON	LOST	PCT.	G	GS	CG	INP	HITS	BB	SO	SH	ERA
14	7	.667	38	28	6	204	170	83	143	1	2.74

Metzger's 1976 Record

WON	LOST	PCT.	G	GS	CG	INP	HITS	BB	SO	SH	ERA
11	4	.733	77	0	0	123	119	52	89	0	2.93

Pat Zachry, who tied for the rookie award in 1976 with Butch Metzger.

Butch Metzger

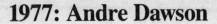

1977: Andre Dawson

"He came to play," was said about the National League's 1977 Rookie of the Year. This is baseball language for a serious, hustling ballplayer, one who doesn't have to look the other way when being handed his paycheck. And they could have added that Andre Dawson stayed to play, for ten years after being voted Rookie of the Year, he was voted the league's Most Valuable Player.

A muscular man who stood 6'3" and weighed 180 pounds, Dawson broke into the Montreal Expos' outfield in 1977 with a .282 batting average. He also hit 19 home runs and played a fine center field. He became Montreal's second rookie winner (after Carl Morton in 1970). With the 23-year-old Dawson flanked in the outer garden by Ellis Valentine and Warren Cromartie, the Expos looked as if they had put together one of the outstanding young outfields in baseball. But of the three, only Dawson was to go on to a long career of stardom.

Dawson's Rookie of the Year selection was a close one—he won by one vote over the New York Mets' young outfielder Steve Henderson, who played two-thirds of the season and batted .297. Dawson had ten votes to Henderson's nine. Getting four votes was San Diego's speedy freshman outfielder Gene Richards, who batted .290 and stole 56 bases. This was a truly impressive rookie year, but it tells us how indelible was the impression Dawson made on the minds of the sportswriters.

Dawson was the complete ballplayer; not only did he hit well and possess a strong throwing arm, but he also ran well.

Andre Dawson

He stole over 20 bases a year during his first seven years in the majors, with a high of 39 in 1982.

In January, 1987, Dawson opted for free agency. He received no offers; nor did some other highly attractive free agents, as the big-league clubs acted in collusion—so ruled an arbiter—to arrest the upward spiral of salaries. Finally Dawson told the Chicago Cubs he would sign a blank contract, letting the club fill in the salary. Under these circumstances, the Cubs could hardly refuse, and they signed Dawson for a half-million dollars, about one third of what he would have received in a free market.

The Cubs acquired quite a bargain, as Dawson bore down and had his greatest year, leading the league with 49 home runs and 137 RBIs and winning MVP honors. The Rookie of the Year of 1977 had made it all the way to the top.

Dawson's 1977 Record

G	AB	HITS	2B	3B	HR	RUNS	RBI	SB	BAV
139	525	148	26	9	19	64	65	21	.282

It is said that there was once a rookie so green that when he heard the coach was out on the field hitting fungos he wanted to know who Fungos was and why they were fighting.

Andre Dawson in 1987, the year he was the National League MVP with the Cubs. He was one of only eight Rookies of the Year who have gone on to win MVP honors.

1978: Bob Horner

There is a baseball proving ground in Tempe, Arizona, that has turned out an impressive number of big league stars—Reggie Jackson and Barry Bonds among them. It is not a part of anyone's minor-league system and, at the end of its four-year season, it hands out a diploma. Arizona State University has for years maintained one of college baseball's most successful and productive programs.

In 1978, Arizona State delivered to the National League its Rookie of the Year, and no rookie could have been more pure rookie than Bob Horner, Atlanta's power-hitting 20-year-old thirdbaseman. Horner, who had been named College Player of the Year by *The Sporting News*, became one of those rare players who vaults over the minor leagues and comes to the majors without any professional experience at all. Rarer still, Horner immediately became one of Atlanta's star sluggers.

Playing just 89 games for the Braves, Horner belted 23 home runs and drove in 63 runs; his home run per at-bat percentage of 7.1 was the best in the league. Abetted by the congeniality of Atlanta's Fulton Stadium to the long ball, Horner was already being labeled as "potentially one of the great home run hitters of all time." With 22-year-old Dale Murphy just beginning to flex his long-ball muscles for the Braves, the team was building an awesome one-two power punch.

When Horner hit 33 home runs in 1979 and 35 in 1980, all of the glowing forecasts seemed to be coming true. After a succession of productive years, the hefty thirdbaseman (who had a tendency to put on weight as easily as some men put on overcoats) began to be plagued by injuries to the extent that he played in only 104 games in 1983 and just 32 in 1984.

After the 1986 season (during which he hit four home runs in a game on July 6), Horner's declaration of free agency fell on deaf ears and he went off to play in Japan. Unable to acclimate to Japan, Horner accepted an offer from the Cardinals in 1988, but injuries ended his work in midseason.

In winning Rookie of the Year honors, Horner pulled 12½ votes to 8½ for San Diego shortstop Ozzie Smith, and three for Pittsburgh righthander Don Robinson. When Whitey Herzog took over as manager of the Cardinals in 1980 and saw Ozzie's glove, he knew what he wanted for Christmas. He got Ozzie in 1982 and with him the team went on to win three pennants.

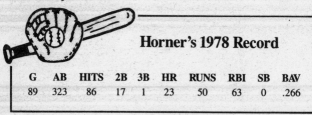

Horner's 1978 Record

G	AB	HITS	2B	3B	HR	RUNS	RBI	SB	BAV
89	323	86	17	1	23	50	63	0	.266

Atlanta's Bob Horner, one of only a handful of men to ever hit four home runs in a game.

1979: Rick Sutcliffe

In 1979, the Los Angeles Dodgers began a remarkable run of four consecutive Rookies of the Year, an achievement no other club has come close to. The first of these was a 6'6", 23-year-old righthander named Rick Sutcliffe, who was to have an unusual peaks-and-valleys career in the majors.

After receiving a reported bonus of $80,000 in 1974, Sutcliffe joined the Dodgers' organization and began working his way toward the promised land. Despite his never having a really big season in the minors, the Dodgers remained high on the big kid with the somewhat stiff-jointed delivery. Sutcliffe pitched one game for the Dodgers in 1976, and Walter Alston, in his 23rd and final year as Dodger manager recalls, "I liked him. He was a big kid, tough, not afraid of anything. And he had good stuff."

Sutcliffe hit the majors to stay in 1979, breaking in with a 17-10 record, and was the runaway winner of the Rookie of the Year Award, getting 20 votes. Finishing second was Houston outfielder Jeff Leonard, a .290 hitter, who received three votes. Leonard later became a star with the San Francisco Giants, where his stolid features earned him one of baseball's more graphic nicknames—"penitentiary face." Getting one vote was Cubs outfielder Scot Thompson.

The 1979 Rookie of the Year took an immediate tumble in 1980, falling to a 3-9 record. Then he descended to 2-2 in 1981, which included some time spent on the disabled list. When Dodger manager Tom Lasorda called Sutcliffe into his office to tell the big guy that he was being cut from the team's post-season play roster, Lasorda suddenly found his office being redecorated in a style known as "Instant Rage." Not surprisingly, Sutcliffe was soon traded, ending up in Cleveland. To many, it seemed more like revenge than a trade.

Sutcliffe prospered on the Cleveland mound, putting in two winning years. In June, 1984, he was traded to the Chicago Cubs, for whom he became a nearly unbeatable, Cy Young Award-winning pitcher with a 16-1 record. Typical of his zigzag career, however, he then turned in a pair of mediocre years before coming back in 1987 with 18 wins, his league-high.

Sutcliffe's 1979 Record

WON	LOST	PCT.	G	GS	CG	INP	HITS	BB	SO	SH	ERA
17	10	.630	39	30	5	242	217	97	117	1	3.46

Rick Sutcliffe, holding a Dodger poster giveaway.

1980: Steve Howe

A new system of selecting a Rookie of the Year went into effect in 1980, based on the Cy Young balloting. The writers picked three players, with the votes allocated 5-3-1 in descending order of preference.

The first National League winner under these guidelines was Steve Howe, 22-year-old lefthanded reliever of the Los Angeles Dodgers. Howe was 7-9, with 17 saves, and a 2.65 ERA. It was a fine beginning for a young pitcher, but in a few years Howe would self-destruct on cocaine and turn his career into a bucket of slop.

By 1984, Howe was under suspension and in rehabilitation. He was back with the Dodgers in 1985, having announced himself cured. But after a series of late arrivals at the ball park, missed games, and a general pattern of shadow boxing in the dark (as well as ineffective pitching), Howe was released. Then the Minnesota Twins took him on, but released him after the season.

Howe's sorry odyssey over the peaks and through the pits took him to the Texas Rangers in 1987. His signing was accompanied by the usual statements of rehabilitation, a clean nose and a new lease on life. He pitched passably well for the Rangers, but then failed a post-season urine test and found himself dumped once more.

Howe's problems had not been without damaging ramifications for the Dodgers. Confident that they had a talented young lefthanded reliever for years to come, the team felt able to trade a similar commodity, and they did—sending John Franco to the Reds in May, 1983, in a trade that netted them nothing and gave the Reds one of the league's best relief pitchers. When Howe's behavior started becoming erratic in 1983, the Dodgers realized that they would soon need another lefty in the pen. Thus, they acquired Carlos Diaz from the Mets in exchange for Sid Fernandez. Diaz fizzled in L.A., while Fernandez became a solid starting pitcher for the Mets. More bad luck.

In the 1980 balloting, eight other rookies followed Howe. Montreal righthander Bill Gullickson had 53 votes; Philadelphia outfielder Lonnie Smith (a .339 hitter), 49; Cincinnati secondbaseman Ron Oester, 16; Houston righthanded-reliever Dave Smith, 13; and there was a scattering of votes among Mets righty reliever Jeff Reardon, San Francisco lefty reliever Al Holland, St. Louis outfielder Leon Durham, and Philadelphia righthander Bob Walk.

Howe's 1980 Record

WON	LOST	PCT.	G	GS	CG	INP	HITS	BB	SO	SH	ERA
7	9	.438	59	0	0	85	83	22	39	0	2.65

Steve Howe, the young man who became his own worst enemy.

Steve Howe

1981:
Fernando Valenzuela

In the spring of 1981, it seemed to have been more or less decided that a big-league player had a definite physical image. Although no one claimed to know exactly what this image looked like, there was no question in anyone's mind that it did not resemble Fernando Valenzuela. As the Los Angeles Dodgers' screwballing young lefthander swept through the National League like an invading army, the baseball fraternity was unanimous in its agreement that he was a most unlikely big-league hero. The 20-year-old rookie from Mexico was on the portly side, carrying what looked suspiciously like a beer belly, and had a plain, expressionless face.

Whatever Valenzuela's appearance was, and whatever it wasn't, the youngster nevertheless possessed a charisma that made him one of the most riveting and talked-about pitchers in a long time. He had become the surest drawing card since Sandy Koufax.

It wasn't just that the roundish young man won, it was how he did it, as well as the aura of pride and dignity he emanated. The great city of Los Angeles simply went wild about him. The whole thing began on opening day, when announced starter Jerry Reuss came up lame and was replaced by Valenzuela. Pitching with the skill and adroitness of a veteran, the 20-year-old screwballed his way to a 2-0 shutout.

From that radiant beginning, Valenzuela went on to win his first eight games, five of them by shutout. By that time, the universe of baseball was beset with "Fernandomania." The Dodger rookie became a magazine cover boy, the most photographed, interviewed, and quoted ballplayer in the land; although the quotes had to come filtered through a Spanish translator—Fernando spoke no English. Dodger manager Tom Lasorda, when asked to account for Valenzuela's appeal, said, "Maybe they see him like a teddy bear and want to hold him, or like a little baby with big cheeks that they want to hug."

The baseball strike, which fractured the 1981 season and cost one-third of the schedule, brought a temporary halt to Fernando's march. Still by the time the season was over, he had posted a 13-7 record, leading the league with eight shutouts and 180 strikeouts.

Some people were wondering if Valenzuela might make a clean sweep of the post-season awards: MVP, Cy Young, and Rookie. As it turned out, he came in fifth in the MVP voting, but won both Cy Young and Rookie of the Year honors. The man he beat out in the rookie voting, 107 votes to 85, was no small potato—Montreal's speedy outfielder Tim Raines. With these two prized rookies dominating the balloting, there was a scattering of votes for New York third baseman Hubie Brooks, Cincinnati righthander Bruce Berenyi, San Diego second baseman Juan Bonilla, Pittsburgh catcher Tony Pena, and New York outfielder Mookie Wilson.

Valenzuela's 1981 Record

WON	LOST	PCT.	G	GS	CG	INP	HITS	BB	SO	SH	ERA
13	7	.650	25	25	11	192	140	61	180	8	2.48

Fernando Valenzuela—no rookie pitcher ever made a more spectacular debut.

Fernando Valenzuela.

1982: Steve Sax

In 1982, the Los Angeles Dodgers broke up their long-time infield alignment of Steve Garvey, Davey Lopes, Bill Russell, and Ron Cey. They traded Lopes to Oakland and replaced him at second base with rookie Steve Sax, who went on to become L.A.'s fourth consecutive Rookie of the Year, following Rick Sutcliffe, Steve Howe, and Fernando Valenzuela.

The 22-year-old Sax, who had started his pro career as a shortstop, made a steady four-year progression through the Dodger farm system, capping his upward climb with a Texas League batting championship (.346) while playing for San Antonio in 1981.

Sax was a spirited, hustling player. His manager Tom Lasorda once said of him, "He plays baseball like my wife shops—all day long." Another teammate said that Steve was the only player who appeared to be looking for still more bases to touch after he had scored.

With the Dodgers losing the division title to Atlanta by just one game that year, Sax batted .282 and led his team with 180 hits and 49 stolen bases.

A few years later, Sax suddenly found himself tormented by an inability to make routine throws to first base. He twice led second basemen in errors, most of them the result of errant pegs. When one writer described Sax's problem as "psychological," an anonymous Dodger pitcher muttered, "it's also a pain in the ass." Sax eventually brought the problem under control.

In becoming the 11th Dodger to win Rookie of the Year honors, Sax narrowly beat out (63 votes to 57) another fine young second baseman, Pittsburgh's Johnny Ray, who batted .281. St. Louis' Willie McGee, a future MVP, was third, followed by San Francisco's Chili Davis, San Diego's right-handed reliever Luis DeLeon, Chicago's Ryne Sandberg (another future MVP), Atlanta's Steve Bedrosian (a future Cy Young winner), St. Louis lefthander Dave LaPoint, and San Diego righty Eric Show. This was an impressive group of rookies.

Sax 1982 Record

G	AB	HITS	2B	3B	HR	RUNS	RBI	SB	BAV
150	638	180	23	7	4	88	47	49	.282

Steve Sax, another of the Dodgers' many star rookies.

1983:
Darryl Strawberry

It is the optimist's credo that there is a bright spot in even the darkest night. Well, in 1979 the New York Mets finished last, entitling them to first pick in the 1980 amateur draft. The young man they reached out for and signed was a tall (6'5"), rangy, and very strong young out-fielder from Los Angeles named Darryl Strawberry. Straw-berry was hardly a discovery—he'd been the apple of many a scouting eye—and it took the Mets a reported $200,000 to coax his name onto a contract. The organization considered it money well spent.

"We penciled him into right field for 1983," one Mets front office executive said. "We figured if this kid wasn't a sure thing, then we might as well close up shop."

They didn't have to close up shop, for the 21-year-old Strawberry was indeed in right field at Shea Stadium in 1983, promoted from the club's Tidewater affiliate soon after the opening of the season. What the Mets were expecting from Strawberry was not a high average but power. Darryl had displayed just that while playing with Jackson in the Texas League in 1982, batting .283 and leading the league with 34 home runs.

There was a certain magic in Strawberry from the very beginning. The tall rookie was an attention-getter, whether he was striking out, stealing a base, or lofting one of his tower-ing home-run shots. He struck out a lot, but the dynamite in his swing was so explosive that in a few years he was consid-ered as intimidating at home plate as Willie McCovey had been two decades before.

After a somewhat slow start, Strawberry gradually adjusted to major-league pitching and began making an impact. Despite averaging one strikeout per game, the tall young man hit 26 home runs and batted .257. After that, the Mets organization settled back to watch their young star get better and better.

Strawberry was an easy winner in the rookie voting, receiving 106 votes. Finishing second with 49 was Atlanta righthander Craig McMurtry, who had a 15-9 record. Chicago outfielder Mel Hall was third, with 32. Following Hall were Cincinnati outfielder Gary Redus, Houston second baseman Bill Doran, Houston lefthander Frank DiPino, Los Angeles first baseman Greg Brock (who had the thankless task of replacing long-time Dodger icon Steve Garvey), Pittsburgh righthander Jose DeLeon, San Diego lefthander Mark Thurmond, and Pittsburgh righthander Lee Tunnell.

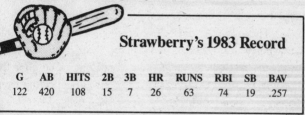

Strawberry's 1983 Record

G	AB	HITS	2B	3B	HR	RUNS	RBI	SB	BAV
122	420	108	15	7	26	63	74	19	.257

Darryl Strawberry—they predicted greatness for him one day.

Darryl Strawberry.

1984: Dwight Gooden

In the summer of 1983, advance word began filtering into sports publications: the New York Mets, the team that had brought Tom Seaver and Nolan Ryan to the major leagues, had another man-sized talent simmering in their farm system. His name was Dwight Gooden; he was just 18-years-old, and he was in the process of buzzing the Carolina League with 300 strikeouts. Those who were cautious by nature pointed out that the Carolina League was not the National League and that, after all, the young man had just completed only his first full season of pro ball.

There were indeed some cautious voices in the Mets' front office when Gooden joined the team in spring training in 1984. No one doubted Dwight's talent, but the feeling among some of the higher brass was that the young man needed one more year of experience in the high minors. There were others who felt that experience was a process, not an end result, and that Gooden was ready. Most vocal among the latter was manager Dave Johnson, and he prevailed.

It was evident from the beginning that Gooden was special. He threw extremely hard and supplemented his speed with a curve that was big, fast and crackling. Both fastball and curve were delivered with an easy, fluid motion.

Gooden fulfilled all expectations in his rookie year. The poised, easy-going youngster helped pitch the Mets to a second-place finish with a 17-9 record and 2.60 ERA. It was his strikeouts, however, that captured the imagination of New York baseball fans. Gooden set a new strikeout record for rookies with 276 in 218 innings (the old record had been Herb

98

Score's 245 for Cleveland in 1955). He also established a new mark (11.39) for strikeouts-per-nine innings (later broken by Nolan Ryan in 1987).

Dwight was an easy winner in the rookie voting, polling 118 votes to 67 for Philadelphia secondbaseman Juan Samuel. Finishing a distant third was Los Angeles' superb young righthander Orel Hershiser. He was followed by San Francisco outfielder Dan Gladden (who batted .351 in 86 games), Gooden's teammate righthander Ron Darling, San Diego outfielder Carmelo Martinez, Philadelphia outfielder Jeff Stone, and St. Louis third baseman Terry Pendleton.

Of the Mets' brilliant young pitcher, it could be said that he wasn't the second coming of Tom Seaver or Nolan Ryan, but the first coming of Dwight Gooden.

Gooden's 1984 Record

WON	LOST	PCT.	G	GS	CG	INP	HITS	BB	SO	SH	ERA
17	9	.654	31	31	7	218	161	73	276	32	2.60

The Mets' Dwight Gooden, who got better and better.

1985: Vince Coleman

Ironically, it was an early-season injury to Cardinal left-fielder Lonnie Smith that enabled Vince Coleman to get into the lineup. Coleman went on to set a new rookie record for steals, with 110, and ran off with the National League's Rookie of the Year Award, and not so incidentally, helping the Cardinals to the pennant. The 24-year-old switchhitter was hardly perfect on the basepaths, however, having been caught stealing 25 times (another rookie record).

Speedy Vince was hardly an unknown quantity to the Cardinals, having led the Appalachian League in stolen bases in 1982, the South Atlantic League in 1983 (with 145), and the American Association in 1984. He repeated as National League leader in 1986 and 1987. With 110 stolen bases in 1985, 107 in 1986, and 109 in 1987, Coleman became the first man in major-league history to steal over 100 bases for three straight years.

In winning the rookie distinction, Coleman beat out (by a 120-72 vote) a very strong contender in Cincinnati lefthander Tom Browning, who was 20-9, the first 20-game-winning rookie in 31 years. Trailing these two top rookies were Los Angeles shortstop Mariano Duncan, San Francisco third baseman Chris Brown, Houston first baseman Glenn Davis, New York reliever Roger McDowell, Pittsburgh outfielder Joe Orsulak, and Montreal southpaw Joe Hesketh.

Coleman's 1985 Record

G	AB	HITS	2B	3B	HR	RUNS	RBI	SB	BAV
151	636	170	20	10	1	107	40	110	.267

Vince Coleman, a near-unstoppable base stealer.

1986: Todd Worrell

Ten different rookies shared votes for Rookie of the Year honors in the National League in 1986, with the Cardinals' big righthanded reliever Todd Worrell getting more than half of them (118).

Built as if he was sculpted in a quarry (6'5" and 215 pounds), Todd possessed the great weapon that is part of the armament of all ace stoppers—the fastball that travels plateward in the high 90's.

Worrell first joined the Cardinals near the end of the 1985 season, but did not accumulate enough innings to invalidate his rookie status for 1986. In '85 he helped pitch the club into the World Series; and a year later, at the age of 26, he became one of the preeminent practitioners of one of baseball's crucial jobs—the short reliever. He appeared in 74 games, won 9, lost 10, and saved 36—the latter a record for a rookie.

Unlike many current relief stars, Worrell hadn't been groomed for the job in the minors. He had been a starting pitcher, one who continued to impress his employers with his blazer, despite his indifferent success. While pitching for Louisville in the American Association in 1985, his manager Jim Fregosi, noting that the big guy began running out of gas by the middle of the game, decided that Worrell's arm had been intended for the shorter haul and assigned him to the bullpen. The transition was made and its wisdom became almost immediately apparent.

Worrell was no less effective in 1987, saving 33 games and again aborting enough crises to help the Cardinals into the World Series. In the '87 Series, Worrell's fastball was clocked consistently in the high 90's, the more batters he fanned, the hotter it got.

Worrell's closest competitor for the rookie award was San Francisco second baseman Robby Thompson with 46 votes. Following Thompson was New York Mets handyman Kevin Mitchell, Houston reliever Charlie Kerfeld, San Francisco's future superstar first baseman Will Clark, Pittsburgh outfielder Barry Bonds, Houston lefty Jim Deshaies, Cincinnati shortstop Barry Larkin, Philadelphia lefthander Bruce Ruffin, and San Diego outfielder John Kruk.

Worrell's 1986 Record

WON	LOST	PCT.	G	GS	CG	INP	HITS	BB	SO	SH	ERA
9	10	.474	74	0	0	104	86	41	73	0	2.08

Todd Worrell, the Cardinals' hard-throwing reliever.

1987: Benny Santiago

There hadn't been a Rookie of the Year catcher since Atlanta's Earl Williams in 1971. By the late 1980s, good defensive catchers who could also hit had become as rare as snow in the Mohave Desert. So when San Diego's 22-year-old Benito (Benny) Santiago appeared on the scene in 1987, it was almost like a revelation.

In the beginning, they talked about Benny's defense more than his hitting. He had an arm, they said, like "a rifle;" and he could fire low, accurate line drives to second base from a kneeling position. Several players, victims of Benny's M-16 pegs, came right out and said they would never try to steal on him again.

By the end of the 1987 season, a prime topic of discussion among baseball men was Santiago's hitting. Not only did he end the season with 18 home runs and a .300 batting average, but from August 25 through October 2, he set a rookie record by hitting safely in 34 consecutive games, a hefty batting streak by any standards.

Santiago's 120 votes for Rookie of the Year (he received all 20 first-place votes) almost doubled the 66 given to the runner-up, Pittsburgh righthander Mike Dunne. The remaining votes were scattered among St. Louis lefthander Joe Magrane, Montreal infielder Casey Candaele, Houston outfielder Gerald Young, Philadelphia outfielder Chris James, Chicago pitcher Lester Lancaster, St. Louis lefthander Greg Mathews, and New York's southpaw reliever Randy Myers.

Santiago's 1987 Record

G	AB	HITS	2B	3B	HR	RUNS	RBI	SB	BAV
146	546	164	33	2	18	64	79	21	.300

Benito Santiago— "the strongest throwing arm in baseball."

106

1988: Chris Sabo

When he went to spring training with the Cincinnati Reds in 1988, Chris Sabo's role had been clearly defined for him: he was going to be the back-up for the club's third baseman Buddy Bell, a veteran and one of the top third basemen of modern times. It turned out to be a classic story of a talented understudy waiting for his chance.

The chance came at the end of spring training, when Bell was injured. Sabo was installed at third base and before long Bell had been dealt to Houston. Chris got off to a fast start—he was the only rookie to play in the All-Star Game—and gave the Reds a spendid all-around year at third base. The 26-year-old speedboy's 46 stolen bases were the most for a Reds rookie since Bob Bescher's 54 in 1909.

Sabo received 79 points in the voting, beating out Cubs first baseman Mark Grace, who had 61. Following were Dodgers pitcher Tim Belcher with 35, Braves infielder Ron Gant with 22, 11 for Padres second baseman Roberto Alomar, and a scattering among Cubs catcher Damon Berryhill, Mets infielder Greg Jefferies, and Phillies first baseman Ricky Jordan.

Sabo's 1988 Record

G	AB	HITS	2B	3B	HR	RUNS	RBI	SB	BAV
137	538	146	40	2	11	74	44	26	.271

Chris Sabo

Before the Award

The Rookie of the Year Award was established in 1947. Of course, there had been some marvelous break-in seasons preceding the Award. Some were turned in by players who went on to become landmark names in baseball history, while others broke in at exalted levels they were unable to sustain. Here are some of the more notable rookie seasons that occurred in the National League before the establishment of official recognition.

1903: Henry Schmidt

It happened a long time ago and not much is known about Henry Schmidt today. A native of Brownsville, Texas, the 29-year-old Schmidt broke in with the Brooklyn Dodgers in 1903. A righthanded pitcher, Henry was an immediate success, ringing up a 21-13 record for a Brooklyn team that finished fifth. Though certainly not a youngster, it looked like he appeared to be setting out on a fine major league career. But he didn't, and today the reasons why are lost in the mists of long ago; for after his excellent rookie season, Henry Schmidt left the major leagues and never returned, leaving behind that one, lone season of rookie excellence.

Schmidt died in Nashville, Tennessee, on April 23, 1926.

Henry Schmidt

1910: Leonard Cole

In 1910, the Chicago Cubs brought into the league's a tall, sad-faced righthander named Leonard Cole, immediately nicknamed "King," after the nursery rhyme character. And Cole was indeed kingly in his rookie year, compiling a scintillating 20-4 record, as he helped pitch the Cubs to the pennant. Cole polished his record with a 1.80 earned-run average, second best in the league.

Cole maintained his mastery in 1911 with an 18-7 record. In 1912, however, he got off to a bad start and the Cubs traded him early in the season to the Pirates. Illness and a sore arm held the former rookie to a 2-2 season. Illness also kept Cole out of baseball in 1913. He was back in 1914, with the Yankees, posting an 11-9 record. In 1915, he was 3-3. On January 6, 1916, Cole died in Bay City, Michigan. He was 29 years old.

Leonard Cole

1911: Grover Cleveland Alexander

In 1911, the Philadelphia Phillies introduced a 24-year-old righthander named Grover Cleveland Alexander to the National League. He was not only an immediate success, but quickly assumed Christy Mathewson's mantle as the league's number-one pitcher. Alex pitched on and on, not retiring until 1930, by which time he had won 373 games, a total that has him tied with Mathewson for "most ever" by a National League pitcher.

Alexander's rookie 1911 record remains the greatest ever logged by a freshman pitcher. The tall, lanky, freckle-faced Nebraskan farm boy rang up an astonishing 28-13 record and 2.57 earned run average, including a league-leading seven shutouts. He fanned 227 batters, which remained the league record until 1984, when it was erased by New York's Dwight Gooden, who had 276.

After the 1911 season, one Philadelphia paper wrote about Alex: "Is he really and truly as good as this, or are we to be disappointed again?" The writer was referring to another Phillies righthander, George McQuillan, who had broken in with a 23-17 record in 1908, but never again came close to repeating that success.

Alex slipped to 19-17 in 1912, but then came roaring back with seasons of 22-8, 27-15, 31-10, 33-12, and 30-13, establishing himself as the unquestionable king of National League pitchers.

After his three consecutive 30-game seasons, Alexander's career was interrupted in 1918 by military service. He served with the American Expeditionary Force in France and saw some heavy action. When he returned, he was an alcoholic and also suffered from epileptic fits. By this time, he was pitching for the Chicago Cubs, for whom he had some fine seasons before being waived to the St. Louis Cardinals.

At the of age of 39, Alexander had his finest moment, against the New York Yankees in the 1926 World Series. In the seventh inning of the seventh game, with the Cardinals ahead, 3-2, Alex, who had pitched a nine-inning victory the day before, shuffled out of the bullpen to fan the Yankees' rookie slugger Tony Lazzeri with the bases loaded. He then went on to preserve the Cardinal lead and nail down the team's first world championship.

Alex played out his days as an alcoholic, a lonely, pathetic figure. He died in St. Paul, Nebraska on November 4, 1950, at the age of 63.

Soon after his death, the one-time rookie sensation had his life brought to the silver screen. The man who portrayed him in the film, "The Winning Team," was Ronald Reagan.

Grover Cleveland Alexander

1922: Dazzy Vance

When he joined the Brooklyn Dodgers in 1922, righthander Dazzy Vance was a 31-year-old rookie who had failed in brief trials previously with the Pirates and the Yankees. But now the days of failure were over for the big, hard-throwing Vance. He broke in with an 18-12 record for the Dodgers in 1922 and led the league with 134 strikeouts, the first of seven consecutive years he led in whiffs.

Despite coming to the majors at the age of 31, Vance, who stayed in the big leagues until 1935, won a total of 197 games, including a high of 28 in 1924.

Dazzy Vance

1930: Wally Berger

The year that 24-year-old Wally Berger came to the big leagues with the Boston Braves—1930—was the heaviest-hitting season in baseball history (the National League as a whole averaged .303). And the rookie outfielder did his share, hitting 38 home runs, which stood as a record for rookies for a long time. Cincinnati's Frank Robinson tied it in 1956, but it wasn't broken until Oakland's Mark McGwire launched 49 home runs in 1987 (Berger and Robinson remain co-holders of the National League record.)

Berger remained one of the league's steadier smashers throughout the 1930s, though sentenced to the Braves, for years a woefully inept team. Wally played until 1940. In 1935, he led the league in home runs (34) and runs batted in (130).

Wally Berger, Opposite

1938: Cliff Melton Lou Fette & Jim Turner

In one of the oddest years of high-class rookie performances, 1938 saw three freshman pitchers turn in 20-game winning seasons in the National League, which would not see another rookie 20-game winner until Cincinnati's Tom Browning in 1985. Making the achievements of this trio even more odd was the fact that none of them ever came close to repeating it.

Melton was a 6'5" lefthander who broke in with the New York Giants with a 20-9 record. He was 25 years old, and the future seemed bright. The following year, however, he dropped to 14-14, and never won that many again. He pitched for the Giants until 1944.

Lou Fette was a seasoned rookie—30 years old—when the right-hander turned in a solid 20-10 record for a fifth-place Boston Braves. And solid it was—Lou hurled a league-high five shutouts and had a 2.88 earned run average. But that was about it for Lou; he was 11-13 in 1938, 10-10 in 1939, and soon after drifted out of the big leagues.

Jim Turner was even older than Fette—33. The right-thander was 20-11, also had a league-high shutouts and led with a 2.38 earned run average. Like Fette and Melton, Turner never repeated that success, though he did pitch in the majors until 1945.

Cliff Melton, Top.   Lou Fette, bot. L.   Jim Turner, bot. R.

Walter Alston, who was Frank Howard's manager when the Gulliver-sized rookie came to the major leagues with the Los Angeles Dodgers, told this story about the enormously strong, good-natured player:

"I guess Frank Howard was just about as big and strong a man as has ever been in this game. We used to have some fun with him on occasion. We brought him up at about the same time we did Tommy Davis and Ron Fairly and a kid named Don Miles. They'd all received pretty good bonuses, and we decided to have a look at them at the end of the year. I put Miles in a game in Chicago, and he crashed into that brick wall and banged himself up. Then in the same game Fairly hit a foul tip off of his toe, and he was out for a few days. Now it was big Frank's turn. We went to Philadelphia. Second time up, he hit a line drive into left field, and as he was rounding first, he tripped over the bag and fell and hurt his leg. So he was out for a while.

After that some of the veterans like Hodges and Reese, who were a couple of pretty good agitators, went into the dressing room and said, "Hey, Skip, they're not putting the stuff into these young fellows like they used to, are they?" They saw Howard on the rubbing table getting worked on—he stuck out over both ends, he was so big—and they brought him a pillow and a glass of water and asked him if there was anything else they could do for him. They enjoyed getting on him because he was sort of easygoing. This went on for four or five days. Then I got Frank off to the side.

"Hey, Frank," I said "Goddamn, you don't have to take

that from them. They're getting a little too rough, don't you think?"

"Oh, no," he said. "It's okay."

"No it isn't," I said. "I think they're going too far. I tell you what you do. Why don't you just take that Pee Wee up and shake him a bit? Gently, of course."

"Pee Wee's a nice guy," he said.

"You listen to me," I said. "They're just going to drive you nuts if you don't quiet them down a little bit."

Then I went over and sat down beside Reese.

"Hey," I said, "I'd sure like to try some more of those kids out. Why don't you get on that Howard and agitate him a little bit and see if I can't get him back into the lineup?"

That suited Pee Wee just fine. I sat back and folded my arms, while he got up and went to the other end of the bench and started needling Frank. Next thing I see is Frank standing up, his back to me, and he's got Reese up off the floor shaking him up and down, and old Pee Wee's arms and legs are flapping and his eyes are shining as big as half-dollars.

Later on Reese came up to me, cussing. "Hey, Skipper," he said, "what's going on?"

"Just having a little fun," I told him.

"Fun?" he said. "I think you're trying to get me killed."

About the Author

Don Honig is one of America's best-known and prolific baseball historians. He is the author of 25 books about the national pastime, including *Baseball When the Grass Was Real*, *Baseball Between the Lines*, *Baseball America*, plus histories of the National League, the American League, the World Series, the All-Star Game, the New York Yankees, the New York Mets and the Los Angeles Dodgers. Mr. Honig is also the author of *The Donald Honig Reader* and has written over 30 baseball titles for young readers. He lives in Cromwell, Connecticut.